Home. It's where the dog greets you at the end of the day. Or where you 'put on the dog' for family and friends. It's full of the noise of people, or it's blissful solitude. It's polished wood, streaming sunlight, tempting aromas from the kitchen. It's heirloom china, soft quilts, bright toys and treasured mementos. It's topiary or vegetable garden, mansion, cottage or duck club, from Halloween to Independence Day.

Private Tour – At Home in Arkansas is a look at the style of the state, from grand to cozy, city to farm. Homeowners have graciously opened their doors and invited us in to see their individual statements of style.

Homeowners on tour, we thank you for your enthusiasm and support! Without your help this book would not have been possible. We dedicate this book to you, to the Junior League of Little Rock, to the Arkansas Easter Seal Society, and to the projects that the sale of this book will make possible.

Private Tour
At Home In Arkansas

Writing and Design by **Hunter W. Gray**

Photographs by **Richard Leo Johnson**

Right: Zanovich – Little Rock
Left: Benton – Helena

THE TOUR BEGINS

Opposite: Hunt – Fayetteville
Below: Wilson – Fayetteville

AT A BEND IN THE RIVER

Dr. Ted and Virginia Bailey have a home on the Arkansas River with a breathtaking view. The Little Rock cityscape stretches out in rich urban profile just across the water. And, on summer days, the river is dotted with colorful watercraft, from sailboats to ski boats, fishing skiffs to barges.

The Baileys see it all from their three-level Georgian style condominium at a bend in the river. The home was built in 1983 as a solution to an empty nest. After raising five children, Ted and Virginia were ready for a new approach to living.

Over the front door is an elliptical fanlight and a multi-paned second story oval window which allow natural sunlight in the foyer. A two-story bay window is draped in yards of deep green fabric with golden trim, focusing even more light on the entrance. A large 30-year-old silk Aubusson tapestry creates a colorful burst of French drama.

The living room is formal, but intimate. One of its visual highlights is a wonderfully ornate wrought iron gated elevator, appointed with gold detailing. What a way to make an entrance! Or choose to sweep down the nearby open staircase with curved banister.

Look up at the massive cornices in this showcase room, which display subtle modillion and dentil detailing, all supported by white Corinthian columns.

Many of the home's detailed accents are golden, from gilt mirrors to the trimmings on period French and English antiques. The Baileys' home presents artwork from across the globe. Styles range from a highly fanciful Oriental vase to framed contemporary posters.

The grace of the home is reflected in the clarity of its millwork, the flair of richly colored Sultanabad rugs and an impressive collection of fine antique books. An end table displays an eye catching cluster of silver bibelots. A richly appointed 18th century cabinet, built in England and finished in China, crests the corner of the living room.

The mood extends onto the inviting outdoor pool area. Entertaining is part of the lifestyle. Cottonwoods, magnolias and river birches sway to the relaxing river breezes at the open poolside.

The Blass architectural firm designed the condominium's exterior and the interior is by Victor Zanovich, ASID, of Little Rock. The woodwork is the masterwork of John Ulmer Builders, Inc.

Virginia was the Junior League of Little Rock Sustainer of the Year in 1979.

THINGS OF BEAUTY

As a 21st wedding anniversary present, Fred Balch gave his wife, Memory, a home that would become a renowned showplace for art and entertainment. The Balch property in Little Rock offers a magnificent display for all that is beautiful.

When Fred was thirteen, he worked at an antique store all summer just to trade the owner for a marble topped table. The desire to collect and live with things of beauty has long been part of his lifestyle.

The Balches believe that a perfectly designed environment is based on English and French adornments with touches of the Oriental. Blending these expressions, Victor Zanovich, ASID, designed three downstairs rooms which feature exotic touches like Fortuny wallcovering and subtly colored fabric draperies. Distinctive custom rugs, bordered with a reed and ribbon motif, provide the backdrop to the many parties the Balches host.

Balch
Little Rock

They like to entertain. And when they pull out all the stops, they often invite David Garner of Marlsgate Plantation fame to fashion the gala. From sculpted linen rosebuds to elaborate floral arrangements to monogrammed petits fours, guests and family members alike are treated to the best. The cherished collection of antique Rockingham china from England is often used. There is also Fred's most cherished possession: a 1790 dinner plate, presented to his great-great-great grandmother by the Marquis de Lafayette, which depicts the original thirteen colonies and stars.

Fred and Memory have an extensive collection of 18th and 19th century pill and snuff boxes. They are carefully hand painted Doré boxes with miniature portraits of court royalty.

Fred started his collections at an early age. When he was five he coveted his Aunt's 18th century miniature (of the same grandmother who received the precious plate). He was eight before he could convince her that the miniature should begin his collection.

The bewitching interior is not the end of the Balch residence's charm. The exterior gardens are carefully arranged and yield colorful dividends during multiple blossoming seasons. The home is surrounded by dogwood, crape myrtle, flowering fruit trees, magnolias and the lighting necessary to convert them to a magical nighttime environment. Memory is a member of the Little Rock Garden Club, but both Balches can be found caring for the gardens.

Those are not goldfish in the pond; they are Japanese koi, or ornamental carp. Bob Sheenhan designed the garden's pool. He built a special road to accommodate the construction project.

A guest cottage was renovated in 1984, replicating a cottage visited on a trip to Bath, England. The country cottage's interior was meticulously appointed by Randall Byars, ASID. The charm includes hand-crocheted bedspreads made by Fred's grandmother.

Fred is the son of the late Fred S. Balch, Sr., and Alberta Rudd Balch. The senior Balch was the 1936 founder of the landmark car dealership, Balch Oldsmobile of Little Rock.

UNDER THE SHADE

Built under the sprawling branches of a magnificent century-old oak is the home of Ferd and Sis Bellingrath.

In planning a home in this Pine Bluff setting, the Bellingraths travelled to New Orleans to look at the work of architect M. McCullar. His home in that city's Garden District served as an inspiration for many design decisions.

This French Colonial home is built in a three-part plan. The two-story center section is flanked by symmetrical single-story wings. In keeping with the period design, the home looks outward. Many rooms have their own exterior entrances with porches. The front door is disguised by two other look-alike shapes that add interest to the entrance. A high masonry foundation is topped by a porch with four simple white columns.

The pool and cabana area were added to the home in 1975 and provide a haven of relaxation.

Ferd's father was a gun collector. His vast collection on display includes wall mounted rifles and a set of prized dueling pistols encased in velvet.

Both children of the family are grown. The interior of the home, however, has undergone few design changes. Its original flow is just as functional as it was when it was conceived in 1961. Sis enjoys attending to her home. She recently has relied upon the talents of Little Rock's Barbi Rushing Interiors to update the home's appointments to match an ever changing lifestyle.

The home has been featured on the pages of *Architectural Digest* and has been included in many local benefit tours.

T I M E L E S S

This interior plays host to antique finds of all sorts – period English furniture, porcelains, chandeliers, sconces, and Oriental rugs. The home of Bill and Helen Benton of Helena is a neoclassic example of timeless beauty.

Helen drew the plans for the original house and for a master bedroom, bath and den addition in 1968. Julia Waggoner from Jackson, Mississippi, helped with remodeling in 1976. Careful attention has been paid to design and materials selection. Only items of the finest quality were chosen.

The large entryway has an unusual Jeffersonian T-shaped front which features decorative molding, Italian tile floor and a prized Waterford crystal chandelier. This foyer was part of the 1976 remodeling, and after a three-year wait, Bill purchased the "one of a kind" chandelier as a surprise Christmas present for Helen. It soon became the focal point of the dramatic entrance.

The chandelier hung without incident for approximately eighteen months. Upon entering the room late one afternoon Helen discovered, much to her dismay, "a million" pieces of shattered crystal on her beautiful tile floor! Faulty installation was the culprit of the disaster. After much searching with the aid of Royal Antiques in New Orleans, where the first chandelier was purchased, another was found almost identical to the original. It presently hangs, securely fastened, in the foyer.

A banquet-size dining room, with custom silk wallcovering from Scalamandré, is filled with antiques. The drawing room has inlaid marquetry floors reflecting intricately carved molding on the ceiling. It also features brilliantly colored fabrics.

The library is not just for reading. It's also used for family entertaining and large group functions because of the tremendous scale: 40' x 29'. The gathering place has a vaulted dome ceiling, and is warmed by soft shades of cream and taupe, with accents of reds and blues borrowed from colors in an Oriental rug and antique porcelain.

A kitchen breakfast area that features faux bamboo cabinet doors, dark green granite countertops and a light cream marble floor is multi-functional with a dining area as well as a comfortable sitting area. In the sunroom, bleached parquet floors and a brilliant rainbow of wall colors overlook a formal garden and pool. There is also a garden room.

The home features all custom baths with marble floors and vanities, one of which has a 20-foot-long skylight. The master suite features separate his and hers baths. Bill's has pickled paneling with a raised ceiling just to accommodate his extra height. Helen's is bright and airy with extra mirrors.

Appointments of crystal and silver are sprinkled throughout the house; family photographs are a favorite accent. A hand-carved wooden mantel is engraved with the Bible verse "Ask, and it shall be given to you; seek, and ye shall find; knock, and it shall be opened unto you." The family has often gathered at the mantel to convey the passage to those leaving on a journey.

Helen's artistic flair shows throughout the home and is also the foundation of her business – she is a designer of wedding gowns, debutante dresses, and other fine clothing. Her bridal designs recently filled all three Fifth Avenue windows of Bergdorf Goodman in New York.

L U C K Y   F I N D

The crisp smells of the Northwest Arkansas countryside are accompanied by the sounds of clear water rushing from a nearby spring. Windows with tiny panes create small squares of light to cascade across dark antique woods. The resulting ambiance is perfect for the rambling log home of David and Karen Buckley.

They were lucky to find this one-of-a-kind home in Springdale. The Rabbit's Foot Lodge is built on its namesake, the Dancing Rabbit Creek of local Indian lore. The creek is filled by a natural spring below the house that yields three million gallons a day! The city of Springdale once used it as a water source.

The home has a rather unusual architectural personality. The roof has a distinctive pagoda look with gently sloping peaks and no gables, and it contrasts sharply with the exposed timbered walls. The main design is true to the regional Ozark Mansion style – a large, rugged, but comfortable house with wide open porches.

To call this a log cabin is an understatement. No doubt it was made from trees felled on the property. The logs were hewn square, then placed horizontally forming massive solid walls of wood. And, in keeping with the style, they were joined at the corners with overlapping saddle notches.

The irregularly spaced concrete grout adds a rustic unstructured feeling to the home. The home took a year to construct and was completed in 1909.

Not much has changed architecturally through the years. However, in the 1970s a cedar-sided addition was added to the rear of the home to screen the basement entry stairs and to house a laundry and game room.

The home is filled with rustic reminders such as carved woodland scenes, animal trophies and colorful native quilts sprawled on family heirlooms.

J. William Fulbright lived in the home from 1934-46 as President of the University of Arkansas at Fayetteville and during part of his early tenure as a U.S. Senator. His personal touches are felt throughout the home and beyond. He built the graceful walkway leading to the source of the natural spring pond.

It is reported that the home was once used to hold town meetings, probably because it was the largest structure in town. The Lodge is a fitting place for the Buckleys' annual Independence Day celebration.

The lodge became part of the National Register of Historic Places in 1985.

Buckley – Rabbit's Foot Lodge
Springdale

COTSWOLD COTTAGE

Styled in the manner of a Cotswold country cottage, the home of George and Margaret Cole is not in the English countryside but inside the city limits of Fayetteville. A small lake on the grounds has been designed to resemble a late 19th century English garden pond. Natural vegetation abounds.

The home is built on the original Butterfield Stagecoach route, on Old Wire Road. In the late 1800s, if mail was routed through here it was stamped with the now famous Butterfield Stage stamp. Old Wire Road was also a route for early telegraph lines.

The original home was built in the 1920s, but a Christmas tree fire in 1979 almost destroyed it completely. A total remodeling was necessary. At that time, an upstairs bedroom suite was expanded, a great room was added, and the guest house was restored. Since then, a pool with a gazebo and hot tub, and a study and dressing room have been added to the complex. The home is constructed so that every room is a corner room with the exception of the master bath.

Margaret is an interior designer and her own home is a continuing project. She claims that it will never be "truly" finished. "There will always be something left to do."

George is an avid sportsman and conservationist who served for seven years on the Arkansas Game and Fish Commission.

George's father, the late George Cole, Sr., was Frank Broyles' predecessor as Athletic Director of the University of Arkansas at Fayetteville. The back bar in the den is the original registrar's desk from Ole Main. You can almost feel the history when you touch the desk.

The great room displays George's Civil War weapons collection and an antique drugstore bar. He is an obstetrician and gynecologist and has collected turn-of-the-century medical equipment. These antiques that were once used in his medical specialty are now used as household furniture and decorative accents.

In the spring, areas surrounding the main house explode with hundreds of jonquils, blossoming crape myrtle, geraniums and lilies. And during the Christmas season, the Coles claim the biggest decorated live tree in Arkansas.

The idea of the perfect Cotswold home was to surround yourself with your favorite things. The Coles have succeeded without exception.

SUMMERTIME IN THE COUNTRY

He was the founder of Arkansas Power & Light Company and, every once in a while, needed to get away from it all. So in 1926 Harvey C. Couch built a lake – and a summer home – in the secluded Ouachita National Forest just outside Hot Springs. The children and grandchildren carry on Harvey's summer legacy.

This rustic retreat stretches out on 114 acres on the banks of Lake Catherine, which Harvey named after his granddaughter. For awhile there

were no phones, but they were later added because of the isolation. Fishing was the original pastime, but Couchwood became much more.

This is a summer home from the time when no one knew how to cool down a hot city kitchen, when entertaining the kids meant swimming in the lake...a place to spend the lazy, hazy days and nights of summer. The family calls Couchwood "nothing fancy, just comfortable."

Not much has changed at Couchwood since it was built. The Couch clan continues the tradition of the annual trek to Couchwood for the season. The kids still find their way down to the lake. And somehow, each summer seems hotter than the one before.

Couchwood has a three bedroom main house and three additional log houses with sleeping quarters. Some of the original wooden beams spanning the main house are so expansive that no trees in Arkansas were large enough and the timbers had to be brought in from the forests of Oregon.

All the houses on the property have their own names: the Big House, and three cabins named Calhoun (you can fish from this one), Remmelwood (Harvey watched it being built from his bed in his last months) and Little Pine Bluff. The estate can accommodate more than 50 people.

Harvey's private train car, the *Magnolia*, was once used to travel across the country in style. It is intact and stands proudly just a few feet from the Big House. It has long since been converted to bedrooms, but remains a reminder of the grand old days of passenger railroads.

It's been said that Couchwood was used to sell Arkansas to the rest of the world. In the Big House is an exposed log wall covered with portraits of dignitaries who have been guests here. This captivating view into history includes pictures of Presidents Franklin Roosevelt and Herbert Hoover, other national and state politicians, and even a snapshot of Will Rogers to name a few. It is reported that in 1936, when President Roosevelt came to pay a visit, "to put on a good front" just the fronts of the buildings were hurriedly painted for his arrival.

Most of the furniture was made on site. Cedar beds and chests add their warmth to this well-visited retreat.

Out the back door of the Big House, toward the lake, is a most unusual bench. It looks like a clever woodsmith has carved out a bench from a huge 60-foot felled tree, but it's actually a stone and concrete replica of a downed oak! The design is by Dionicio Rodriguez who was made famous by his design of the Old Mill in North Little Rock.

Couchwood has recently been modernized with central heat, air and city water. It really has remained a family summer place for all these years.

SOUTHERN OASIS

It's hard to see through the cypress trees on Lake Enterprise in south Arkansas near Wilmot. But at the edge of an oxbow lake, the soft lacy green curtain of Spanish moss lifts to reveal the home of John and Bland Currie.

Surrounded by cotton fields is an oasis of finery on a lush knoll. John and Bland both grew up in the area. The land is a fourth generation working farm with more than 2,500 acres of cotton in production. The Curries also own a local farm equipment store.

Their home was built in 1983 and is a classic French design. Bay windows at the rear of the home frame wonderful views of the cypress-lined lake. If you go down to the water's edge, you will probably be greeted by the family hounds.

Hipped roof lines echo the French colonial design. With all the moss hanging from the cypress trees, you're compelled to imagine an earlier time when French settlers were migrating up the mighty Mississippi Delta. Their design influences can be felt in many of the home's features. There are numerous exterior doors and the simple narrow casement windows have paired shutters. Most of the windows are clean designs without coverings. The front door is framed by simple fanlights.

In the living room, the distinctive, unpretentious planked ceiling adds charm. Yet the contrasting textures of starkly modern chrome and leather chairs designed by Ludwig Mies Van Der Rohe fit right in. An unexpected green Italian marble fireplace commands the entire room.

A cherished authentic Irish hunt table adorns the other end of the room. When the hunters ate breakfast, the drop leaves were extended and the table was filled with food and carried into the field. The gamesmen ate heartily without fear of tracking mud into their clean homes.

The 1880 English chandelier in the dining room was purchased in New Orleans. It sets the right mood for a scrumptious meal prepared by the Curries, who both like to cook, and have a kitchen to match their culinary interests and expertise.

Another glimpse of this wonderful oasis home is featured on the back cover of this book.

NEW, WITH CHARACTER

You would never guess that this home is only three years old. Filled with touches that take a lifetime to collect, the home of Delmar and Cheri Edwards of Fort Smith took five years to plan.

A medieval style facade greets the tour with quarry-faced limestone veneer, imported from Kansas. French eclectic arched top dormers give a taste of elegance with contrasting stone facings.

Guests are welcomed inside by a jutting gabled portico that beckons the visitor to open the handmade lead crystal French doors. Cheri helped design the pattern. From there you can practically see it all...two-and-a-half floors open all the way to the ceiling with winding staircases.

Every detail has been thought out, from a mirrored exercise room in the master suite to the cheery white sunroom that looks out on a small lake. Residents of a martin house herald spring each year.

The kitchen is built around a hefty French butcher block table purchased in New Orleans. There is even a working kitchen fireplace.

Delmar's study is a gentleman's fancy. The custom cabinetry and river-grain mahogany paneling are traditionally crafted and contrast well with the open beamed ceiling. And, proudly on display above the well-appointed bar, is the winning pigskin from a Razorback football game. A traditional wardrobe has been converted to a bar, and its sink sports a refurbished antique English copper tap.

The master bathroom can be adapted to fit the mood. A sunken black Jacuzzi is counterpoint to a towering white marble three-sided fireplace. Wood for the fireplace is cleverly hidden inside the marble. The sun pours through an expansive clerestory skylight.

In a small powder room downstairs, glimpse a hand painted porcelain Italian Renaissance sink and a gracefully carved Chinese screen which divides the room.

The family room warms guests with a fireplace dating from the 1880s; the mantel is crafted from solid walnut, and an antique French firescreen stands at the hearth.

At Christmas the Edwards decorate their home with tasteful exterior lighting and cheerful inside touches including banisters wrapped with colorful ribbons and pine boughs. A full-size antique sleigh from Durango, Colorado, is on display, complete with presents.

No matter the season, their home is always brimming with light, from within and without. Tim Rizley of Fort Smith is the architect.

GET AWAY FOR GOOD

It was built to be a summer home, a weekend retreat and a hunting lodge, and for two years that's just what it was...a great getaway on the outskirts of North Little Rock.

However, Herschel and Beth Friday found the setting, the peace and quiet, and the livability so irresistible that they gave up city life and moved out to the Bob White Hill Ranch full-time.

The 330 acre estate includes their home, a guest house, a tennis court, an air strip, stables, and a swimming pool...but no neighbors. It offers a perfect panorama of the valley; it was planned that way. The Fridays bought enough surrounding land to maintain their view of forest and field, so they could hear nothing louder than birds chirping and grass growing.

The log-constructed main house is rustic, but with a bit of polish. It was actually purchased as a kit home. The rooms are large and simple, and

instead of a doorway, transitions are indicated by a step from one Oriental rug to another. The "ranch" offers all the comforts of the Fridays' former home in west Little Rock, without the formalities of interior walls and woodwork.

The peaked ceilings are paneled and feature rough-hewn log beams. The living room casually displays tufted leather sofas and chairs and portraits of family members. A native stone fireplace flanked by oak bookshelves divides this welcoming area from the dining area. Knickknacks and collectibles are proudly displayed. A lamp from the original Oaklawn Jockey Club shines over the informal dining room table; Herschel is on the board of the famous Hot Springs racetrack.

The upstairs bedrooms are simple spaces with perfect details – warm, wood-paneled walls, museum-quality quilts, leather-bound books.

The home is big enough for just about any kind of entertaining the Fridays could dish up, and friends are always ready for a trip to the country.

Soon after completion of the home in 1984 the Fridays added a carriage house, complete with storage and a two-bay airplane hanger. Herschel plays an active role in his law firm with offices in downtown Little Rock, but he never has to face the traffic on the river bridges. He flies his plane into Adams Field on workday mornings!

Herschel was the 1989 recipient of the Arkansas Easter Seal Society's Arkansan of the Year Award, recognizing his commitment to the community.

EPIC PROPORTIONS

Just east of Little Rock is the sleepy little community of Scott. A two-lane highway winds its way through cotton fields and old hardwoods, and up to Marlsgate Plantation, where the Old South comes alive.

This stately Delta plantation house was built in 1888. The house has overlooked a working plantation for most of its existence.

In 1986 David P. Garner, Jr., purchased the home and began extensive restoration. The Little Rock designer Victor Zanovich, ASID, has played a major role in restoring the home to its splendor.

Marlsgate is surrounded by working cotton fields and a pecan orchard. Many of the flowers used to brighten the interior are grown on the grounds, as are many of the foods used at catered occasions.

Garner – Marlsgate Plantation
Scott

The rear verandah looks out on Bearskin Lake. During the spring and summer, the public is treated to special concerts on the lawn. A winter backdrop reveals the starkness of the home's architectural beauty.

The fires are still built and fanned by hand; the linens are still cooled before ironing. The new gardens were designed by P. Allen Smith of Birnam Wood Nurseries, Ltd., of Little Rock. Walking through the garden reminds you of a genteel lifestyle from a century ago.

There are six upstairs bedrooms, all appointed and furnished in the classic pre-Civil War style with soft creams, rich Confederate grey and deep hues of maroon seen in upholstered furniture and formal window coverings.

Rare antebellum furnishings reflect the period from 1830-1860. Fine 18th and 19th century landscape and portrait studies add a sense of heritage.

Garner – Marlsgate Plantation
Scott

A music room makes its presence known, if not by sound, then by the prominence of a grand piano and an exquisite full-size harp.

Glistening one-of-a-kind crystal chandeliers highlight ornate relief designs in plastered ceilings. Other ceilings are adorned with detailed impressions in hammered tin.

David and Marlsgate were recently featured in *Catering Today*. David, whose specialties include floral design as well as catering, explains that "my hobby is my business, and my business is my hobby." Marlsgate offers a showcase for both talents and allows David the perfect business environment as well as a grand home. Today, parts of the home are used for private gatherings, giving guests the opportunity to experience the past. When it's time to entertain foreign dignitaries, or host the perfect celebration in grand style, Marlsgate is first on the list. It has been the setting for numerous weddings, lavish receptions, and many a debut. This home is truly an experience of epic proportions.

Placed on the National Register of Historic Places in 1975, Marlsgate has been featured in numerous local and national publications.

I N S I D E   O U T S I D E

Flagstone seamlessly transcends from inside flooring to outside deck areas. Glass walls summon the visitor to take the terraced walk down to the river. Love of the outdoors is very much a part of the restful interior of the woodsy retreat of Jack and Mollie Grober which overlooks the Arkansas River in Fort Smith.

The native stone construction is anchored by a mammoth fireplace, centered in a 40-foot row of clerestory windows. Moss is encouraged to grow on the massive stone mantel, furthering the illusion of the outdoors within.

Lighting throughout the home is natural by day with direct task lighting at night. Dramatically placed spotlights illumine art and selected architectural features.

Stacked stone columns and another massive fireplace set the master bedroom's mood. The bedcovering is a "Frank Lloyd Wright inspired" tropical leaf print, with Kenyan batik floral print draperies, giving the room an exotic air. Open closets are out of sight, yet conveniently located just behind the tall headboard. Beyond the closets are twin dressing areas. Next is a large sunken tub, flanked by two showers with unexpected sunny skylights.

The home is centered around two kitchens for entertaining. Granite countertops highlight the main designer kitchen, with elevated areas that overlook the living and dining rooms. The molding-mounted light fixtures are made from the same wood as the rest of the accents. The second kitchen, called a small "cleanup kitchen," is less formal and more convenient. It is perfect for the casual, small group entertaining that the Grobers enjoy frequently.

Warm wood tones are reinforced by the colors of the understated furnishings, accented judiciously with animal print pillows, a bear rug and weathered metal candle holders.

E. Fay Jones, FAIA, the nationally renowned architect, designed the home for the Grobers in 1987. His detailing, fondness for built-ins and outward orientation are very much a part of this fabulous home.

Grober
Ft. Smith

VIEW OF HISTORY

This Helena Delta home has been in the family for more than 150 years. It has seen the furor of Civil War, the excitement of Mississippi riverboat races and the splendor of Old South weddings.

Estevan Hall was originally built by Fleetwood Hanks in 1826 and is the modern-day home of his great-granddaughter, Katherine Stephens Hill. A family friend named the home "Estevan Hall," inspired by the tales of an adventurous Spanish prince named Estevan. Stephens is Katherine's maiden name, which translates to Estevan in Spanish.

The slower lifestyle of a bygone era is reflected in the antebellum architectural and landscaping details. Sweeping full-facade verandahs set the stage. Summertime banana trees frame the front pillared porch and magnolias dot the lawns, adding gentle aromas. Crowley's Ridge, the famous Civil War and natural dividing landmark, encroaches the yard.

Although the home shows the touches of five generations, the original layout has been maintained. Much of the window glass throughout the home is original. The sun-drenched breakfast nook looks out on Crowley's

Ridge. And arched French doorways line the front, a detail echoed by arched dormers on the upper floor.

Proud times are on display. Filled with memorabilia, the living room shows off every facet of family history. An upright glass case contains a Civil War cannonball, the crest from a Southern standard, and even a carefully preserved lock of hair.

Judge James Millinder Hanks, the son of the original owner Fleetwood Hanks, recorded history from 1865-1909. His diaries rest on a very simple bench-style desk from the home's early days. The Judge was a U.S. Congressman, and is credited with securing a grant to build the University of Arkansas at Fayetteville. The diaries tell of the historic 1870 riverboat race between the Robert E. Lee and the Natchez. Imagine the thrill of watching from the verandah!

Parts of Estevan Hall are available for tours throughout the year. The home has opened its doors and lawns to many weddings, including Helen Keller's grandparents in 1845. They were married in front of the fireplace in the living room.

The upstairs is filled with fine examples of beautiful antebellum and Victorian furnishings. Period quilts and crisp bed linens adorn museum-quality furniture.

Estevan Hall is on the National Register of Historic Places. It's one of the few standing examples of Delta architecture.

Hill - Estevan Hall
Helena

EASTERN INFLUENCES

Towering southern pines whisper in the breeze on a wooded site with a view of the Ouachita Mountains. The Far East meets the mid-south in the spacious multi-zoned home of Joe and Cheryl Howe.

The simplicity of Japanese elements are fused with Arkansas tradition. The "post and beam" style of Frank Lloyd Wright combines with scored gable facings and pagoda roof curves. The home occupies over 4,000 square feet, with a greenhouse and a two-story workshop and office nearby.

This quasi-Japanese style home spent two years on the drawing board of Hot Springs architect David French. The attention to detail shows in every facet of the home. After the five year planning stage, the Howes were actively involved in the home's year-long construction. Joe is an avid woodworker. He made the pulls for the kitchen cabinets and assisted in producing some of the intricate eastern-style eaves.

Shoji screens in the dining room and Shoji screen-type cabinetry fronts in the kitchen visually speak the language of focused simplicity. Less is better, and each detail is appreciated more.

Simple inset borders with contrasting woods frame the stairways. Take the twisting turns from one level to the next – light and art grace irregularly shaped wall sections. Vantage points are staged from landings. Your point of view is as important as what you are looking at.

The entire house is a formidable art gallery, with sculpture by the Parisian artist Jeanfo, who now resides in Hot Springs. Surprises abound around every curve. Art becomes one with the environment. For instance, a canoe might seem out of place in anyone else's living room, but here it works. The sleek handmade cedar-strip craft is mounted on the wall just above the exterior windows, echoing the designer's use of woods and shapes in the home. The canoe was purchased from the Canadian exhibit at the 1984 World's Fair in New Orleans.

The high sheen of clear lacquered flooring allows the grain of perfectly matched white oak and stained mahogany walkways to shine. The flooring was designed and constructed with such care that you might imagine you are walking on fine furniture.

All year long, colorful orchids grow in abundance inside a specially designed greenhouse just a few feet from the house.

Sparse furnishings stand out against curved walls — architectural appointments are brutally involving. Subtle colorations of soft greys and the simple unadorned starkness of the style make the home itself a work of art.

SMOOTH AND ELEGANT

The sprawling, 350 acre estate of J.B. and Johnelle Hunt near Fayetteville is unpretentious splendor. From the pleasant curve of arched windows and doorways throughout the home to the built-in conveniences and relaxing pool, the feeling is smooth and elegant.

The estate includes three other buildings: a 6,000 square foot workshop, a 1,700 square foot second house, and a 15-stall stable with tack room.

Remote controlled, custom wrought iron gates mark the approach to the main house, centered on acres of manicured lawns. The home was built in 1986 in classic French country, Adam revival style.

The sweeping elliptical fanlight shape, echoed throughout the home, begins above the front doors and is repeated in the wood paneling above the living room fireplace and in entrances to rooms off the main hallway. At the front of the home, Pella Palladian casement windows topped with the half-ellipse fans continue the theme. All windows are shuttered.

A highly polished marble floor greets guests at the main entrance. Above is a custom crafted chandelier. The entire first floor features gracious ten-foot ceilings.

The Hunts each have a private domain within the home. His study is texturally rich and comfortable, with deep inset ceiling panels and walnut walls. Built-ins hide file drawers, a computer and fold-away workspace. The desk is highlighted by small spotlights.

Johnelle's fabulous kitchen is well worth a visit, even if you're not hungry. It includes a fireplace and chaise lounge for relaxing. The ceramic tile floor has a contrasting border which extends to the fireplace surround. Some of the cabinets have beveled glass inserts; others have raised panel walnut faces that match the doors of the double-wide Sub-Zero refrigerator. Countertops are white Corian. A three-compartment sink with an automatic hot water dispenser makes any entertaining occasion a breeze. Relax in front of the fireplace on a white upholstered chair and ottoman, draping your shoulders with a warm afghan.

This home has remarkable features like door-activated lights in the walk-in closets and instant hot water at all fixtures.

When the Ozark mountain air is crisp, the Hunts can rely on their three fireplaces for a feeling of warmth. During warmer months, the 6,000 square foot pool area is the center of attention. Under a roofed terrace, quarry tile spills down to an open air terrace level made of brick, which descends to the decked pool area. A wooden gazebo houses a full entertainment center and conceals the pool equipment.

The Hunts are founders of J.B. Hunt Transport, Inc., the successful trucking firm. J.B. and Johnelle are the joint recipients of the Arkansas Easter Seal Society's 1990 Arkansan of the Year Award.

EXQUISITE INFORMALITY

Keith James is an early morning thinker. One morning, while nibbling cantaloupe, he pondered what color to paint the walls of his Little Rock condominium. It occured to him that his breakfast provided the answer, so he took the melon to the paint store to make the perfect match.

The warm glow of this color scheme provides a lovely backdrop for Keith's collection of French and contemporary art. Keith, an interior designer, doesn't feel the pressure of his work at home. He is quick to point out that things are not carefully arranged. And he's not bound to formality when choosing objects to decorate his home. His Elvis Presley clock is a perfect example. Another is a set of two Donald Roller Wilson paintings of monkeys in children's clothing.

Keith has maximized the impact of precious square footage. He has taken the home's scale into account in making every decision. Small lamps with tiny bulbs warm the darker corners. A petite footstool is nestled under the coffee table. Many times, a large item is echoed in miniature. For instance, a spectacular floral arrangement may be answered visually by a single bloom in a doll-sized vase.

Flowers are very important to the home's mood and appear in virtually every room in arrangements large and small. When Keith returns from travelling, he has the house furnished with flowers from his most recent destination to make the transition easier.

Elegant finishes surround guests. A remarkable mixture of French and contemporary furniture, and fabrics of cream, salmon and taupe complete the setting. One of Keith's favorites is a chair upholstered in exotic silk tiger velvet, an example of his gift for perfection in detail.

WINGS OVER THE PRAIRIE

Many have hunted the duck-abundant wetlands of eastern Arkansas, but only a few have hunted at the world-renowned Wingmead just outside of Roe. Only a few have experienced the charm of its aristocratic nuances, its attention to the details that make up the perfect traditional hunt.

Back in 1938 Edgar Monsanto Queeny, founder of the Lion Oil and Monsanto Corporations, conceived and built the ultimate hunting and wildlife habitat. The name "Wingmead," of Scottish origin, translates as "meadow of wings."

Wingmead's owner doesn't just oversee some wetlands with a house, but takes on the role of conservator – of curator and preservationist of the natural abundance. And after the passing of Mr. Queeny in 1977, Frank and Laura Jane Lyon took on that role with the purchase of Wingmead. The Lyons have always been active in wildlife conservation and Frank is a past chairman of the Arkansas Game and Fish Commission.

Not many things have changed over the years at Wingmead. Hunters are still helped out of their muddy boots by the staff. A "Model 12" shotgun might be handed to you as if by a golf caddy. This is hunting with all the finery – the spirit of the hunt is alive and well at Wingmead. At the end of the day, the table is set with fine china embellished with the recognizable Wingmead logo.

Surrounding the 10,000 square foot antebellum plantation style main house are working farmlands. Rice and soybeans rule these parts. The land includes more than 12,000 protected acres along with a 4,000 acre reservoir with a levee two miles long, providing just the right habitat for waterfowl.

Edgar was always intrigued by flight and, at the inception of Wingmead, he hired aeronautical engineers and biologists to study the duck flyways. Many of their findings helped develop sound conservation methods for use at Wingmead and along the entire Delta flyway.

Art is in abundance at Wingmead. There is a complete duck stamp print collection, cut crystal etched by Richard Bishop, and walls lined with photos capturing the excitement of past hunts. You'll find carved duck logos, light switch plates that have wildlife scenes, and carpeting with depictions of ducks in their natural environment. But the hunt isn't over with the close of duck season. Deer, turkey, quail and some of the best fishing around provide the avid sportsman with year-round adventure. A jet landing strip is on the property for those quick getaway weekend hunts.

Wingmead has been featured in *Town & Country* and many television programs including the widely distributed Ducks Unlimited 1950s documentary "Wings over the Prairie."

Lyon – Wingmead
Roe

GENERATIONS

Seven oaks shade the McCrary homestead near Lonoke. Filled with the memories of four generations, this spacious home was built in 1913 for the maternal grandparents of L.C. McCrary III, state Senator Charles A. and Annie Walls. The holiday gathering place of the clan, which included statesman and uncle Joe T. Robinson, it is now the home of Carolyn McCrary, wife of the late L.C. McCrary III, and her daughters Charlotte and Caroline.

When the home was built on the Lonoke prairie, the yard was treeless. Charles Walls added the oaks, now grown tall. The home follows a Greek revival plan and features a white Tuscany columned facade. Columns are a recurring theme throughout the Charles L. Thompson design. They frame interior doorways and the carriage house which is connected to the main house by a colonnade.

The house is a showcase for the McCrary collections. Throughout the home are fine examples of the family's taste for Western art, Native American art, wildlife art, oil paintings, European antiques and Oriental rugs.

Downstairs, the wine cellar, formerly the site of the coal-fed boiler which heated the house, offers a cool retreat. In addition to the wine itself, the area serves as a storm cellar, and displays a collection of corkscrews and a commanding statue of the god of wine and revelry, Bacchus. L.C. McCrary's grandmother, Annie, once fermented special wine to serve at her daughter's wedding.

Other buildings on the grounds included a two-room servant's house, a separate outdoor restroom, and a large storage building with the front partitioned off and screened in for a chicken run. There was once a tennis court on the back lot.

The main house originally had nine rooms. The attic was floored, and the basement housed the furnace which heated the radiators throughout the house. The family has undertaken two major renovations. In 1946, the L.C. McCrary, Jr. family moved in the home. They extended the porches to allow more interior space, and added a three-car parking area, and installed extensive landscaping.

In 1977 and 1978, Carolyn and her husband added a north wing, which includes a game room, a garden room, and a utility room. All porches were enclosed and central heat and air were installed.

The chandelier is the original dining room fixture and the grand piano has been in the home for three generations. The woodwork throughout the interior was once stained dark mahogany, but has been brightened with paint the color of golden oak. Once known for its 300 Darwin tulips, the north side garden area is now filled with the blaze of azaleas.

The home has seen occasions grand and small. The attic has been used by daughters for a dance studio. The first Miss Arkansas, Imogene Schneider, was received at a gala during the state's Centennial. This lovely setting has been the site of several senior proms.

Placed on the National Register of Historic Places in 1982, the McCrary home has been a favorite family destination and has seen generations of Christmases, Thanksgivings and weddings.

LAVISH SHELTER

It was built in 1950 as a bomb shelter – the first above ground concrete residence in Arkansas. But the home of Little Rock designer Bruce McEntire, ASID, is full of warmth. It's an intimate home, filled with remarkable art and antiques.

The design makes extensive use of glass blocks to allow natural lighting. Above is a flat roof, trimmed with copper. Harry Wongler, architect for the original Arkansas State Capitol, was in his 80s when he conceived this unusual home.

In the dining room, colors from a Gracie hand painted silk are borrowed to set the mood of the room – salmon for wall color and soft green for the ceiling. On the dining table, gladioli stand at attention in crystal vases. Also in view is an unusual English silver venison serving dish. The candelabra are Matthew Bolton designs.

In the living room on the grand piano is a bronze of Napoleon, depicting the monarch at the battle of Waterloo. The room's walls are lacquered a terra cotta color and the ceiling is richly painted in chocolate brown. Oil paintings from the 18th and 19th centuries, including an impressive array of landscapes one of which is an Old Dutch, are embellished with wonderfully elaborate frames – the ornate gilt is mesmerizing.

Collectibles of all descriptions abound. From his trips abroad, Bruce has brought home many a bauble. The perfect way to display them is on an 1860s English rosewood table with bronze roping. The table shows off treasures which include Waverly novels, a German music box, crystal, marble and alabaster eggs, and silver pill boxes. Nearby on another table is a highly polished silver butler's notepad complete with pocket chain.

Napoleon would be flattered by this collector's paradise; there is a room named after him. His likeness is depicted on every conceivable object including oil portraits of him as a young man, sketches, figurines, busts, even dining plates which include Josephine – they all seem to announce the arrival of the French dignitary.

The daybed, Empire chest and a French marble and bronze table were purchased in Paris. A French hooded chair is positioned next to an elaborate screen that has touches of 14 karat gold. There is a luxurious papered ceiling border of medallions holding draped painted silks. The idea is repeated in the reading room with a border showing colorful floral garlands, ornaments and figurines from the 19th century.

COLONIAL TREASURE

Like walking back in time, this home delights the senses with rich tones and textures from another century, yet this home was built in the 1930s to reflect the mood and lifestyle of an age gone by.

Known as Oakland, the two-story Southern Colonial home is owned by Dr. Robert and Dianne Murfee. Oakland was built on a ten-acre tract for Dianne's grandparents, Dr. and Mrs. Garland D. Murphy, Sr., and was named after Dr. Murphy's birthplace in Union Parish, Louisiana.

Modern conveniences don't intrude on the nostalgic mood. The Murfees prefer the glow of candlelight to electric bulbs in the more formal rooms. Rustic detailing on the porches keeps the focus on the past.

The appointments are rich in every room. Decorations maintain the Colonial style of architecture, and each room is filled with American and English antiques dating from the 18th and 19th centuries. Some are original hand-me-down family furnishings. Dianne designed and stenciled, in true 18th century fashion, the intricate 9' x 12' dining room floorcloth.

The kitchen has a working wood-burning, open-hearth fireplace, designed in the 18th century "keeping room" style. Homey aromas of baking breads and pumpkin pie fill the air every fall. The hand-cut exposed beams were

Murfee – Oakland
El Dorado

obtained from the New Hampshire Historical Society and are now adorned with an ever-expanding woven basket collection.

The chief architect was Dave Weaver of El Dorado Lumber Company, and Preston A. Dearing of El Dorado was the builder. The walls are built of solid wood, and the flooring was crafted from white oak, all local virgin timber.

The bricks for the foundation and living room fireplace are red El Dorado scratch brick made by the El Dorado Brick Works. The box columns on the front portico are also the work of local craftsmen.

An upstairs bedroom features a faithful reproduction of an antique doll house, built for the Murfee daughters in 1974. The Murfee collection of quilts includes one discovered only a few years ago which was made for ancestors going off to the Civil War.

This home, decked with charming handcrafted seasonal decorations, is a favorite on the El Dorado Service League's Christmas Tour of Homes.

S W E E T H E A R T   D R E A M S

When she was fifteen and he was seventeen, they stood side by side and vowed they would someday build their dream home on forested land outside El Dorado. In 1985 Michael and Sydney Murphy's dream came true. Rising from 30 heavily wooded acres on the outskirts of town is the realization of their vision – formal yet comfortable, outdoorsy yet refined.

Assembling all the pieces of the dream has taken a lot of energy. Extensive travel has allowed the Murphys to experience many forms of architecture.

They have observed cultures from the exotic to the traditional, with architectural treatments that range from whimsical to sedate. Whether they gathered material swatches, bold artwork, or even articles and photos from magazines, all their ideas ended up influencing the final feeling of their home in the woods.

The home, with overhanging tile roofs and stucco walls, is patterned after the pool pavilion at the Sandy Lane Hotel in Barbados. There are one-

room-wide wings with cross-ventilation between the pool on one side and tree-lined meadows on the other, creating an airy atmosphere.

Sydney is an gifted interior designer whose work at one point in her career was almost totally traditional. Now she prefers the earthtones of Southwestern art, bold colorful contemporary prints, and surprise touches, like mixing in bronze Fu dogs as fireplace sentries. Picasso, Pissaro and Seurat set the mood in other areas. The result is a clean-edged eclecticism, a sensation that is dramatic and sweeping.

Each piece of furniture and artwork in the Murphy home is remarkable in itself. In the living room, a fanciful pot by R.C. Gorman casually rests on the hearth, and high above the mantel, a framed niche presents a work by Dallas artist David McCullough. A Jean Dufy painting rests over the mantel in the bedroom.

Alcoves show off everything from fine art collectibles to the Murphy children's masterpieces. The atmosphere is easy, open and very fluid, with no visually hard surfaces. Textures and colorations borrow from the outdoors. And outdoors is where the focal point of the home is found.

Massive Roman columns announce the pool pavilion area. Large Italian terra cotta pots hold festive flowers. And soft chaise lounges invite you to linger at the poolside. The pool and terrace were initially built with guests in mind, but the family soon developed a lifestyle which demanded more frequent use.

HOME IN BLOOM

Their home is alive with flowers year 'round. John and Rosanna Purdy are the second generation owners of a flower and gift shop in Newport. They definitely bring their work home with them, from the luxury of fresh blooms daily in the dining room to the array of intricate silk arrangements throughout the home.

The Colonial French style home has a very distinguishing high-hipped pavilion roof and a pillared porch that stretches the length of the facade. Bright white square-cut spindle railings along the brick porch evoke the charm of old Louisiana. The relaxed style is just what John and Rosanna wanted when they designed their home together.

Rosanna is partial to combinations of blue and white; many blue and white contrasting wallcoverings and fabrics are present throughout the home. There is an extensive collection of ceramic vases and bowls in the living room, and hand painted blue and white antique plates and serving dishes are carefully hung in the foyer. Even the front door is azure in hue.

The house is spacious and restful, with the Purdys' many collections adding interest to the nooks and crannies. In the dining room, Hummel figurines and Lalique crystal are proudly displayed in multi-paned glass-fronted cabinets.

In designing and decorating their multi-story home, the Purdys paid great attention to details such as the woodwork. They rescued antique orna-mented door facings for use in their home. Some feature carved birds, others have thistles. The spacious master bedroom has custom woodwork.

John and Rosanna live in every inch of the home that they built in 1979. They like visitors, and when the college-age children come home, they always bring friends.

Settle into one of the numerous chair groupings located in just the right places. From the comfortable family room to the breezy porch, it's easy to stay for awhile in Newport.

L I G H T   S T R O K E S

Sunlight pervades the home of Jim and Jane Tinnin, creating a springtime air year 'round. With summer and winter porches and comfy sitting areas framed by windows, sunshine is a part of the decor and part of the life of this home.

This rambling 10,000-plus square foot country estate was built on a 50 acre site just outside Fayetteville in 1988. The architect, Rene Diaz, has beautifully employed the Hampton style.

An airy grace flows from room to room in this very open atmosphere. Jane worked closely with the Dallas interior design firm of Wilson & Associates and played a major role in many of the design and decor decisions. For example, she knew exactly what dining room chairs she wanted built; she had saved the design for fifteen years in her idea notebook.

The front hall runs the entire length of the home. Just off the main hallway, a wonderful kitchen makes a major visual statement with its black and white check marble flooring and lavish green marble countertops. Miniature floodlights, mounted in a white beamed ceiling, are aimed at the marble work surfaces. Multi-paned glass cabinet doors echo the exterior windows.

The wooden floors are *trompe l'oeil* works of art, hand painted by Suzanne Kittrell. The beautifully detailed foyer "rug" even has fringe depicted at either end. Bunny rabbits and playful foxes dance up and down the staircase that leads to the children's rooms. And, in an upstairs little girl's bedroom, the floor has a painted border of whimsical ribbons that meet in a bow.

The master bedroom gets its main sunlight from a detailed Palladian window to the south. The high pitched roof lines are emphasized by fanciful ceiling trusses emulating the fan of the Palladian style transom.

The drive onto this estate is breathtaking. The rolling hills of Northwest Arkansas and bright white planked fencing frame this gem of the Ozarks. But you've already been there! This view is proudly displayed on the cover of this book.

NATURALLY CONCEALED

On the top of a hill, overlooking the crystal blue waters of Greers Ferry Lake, is a vacation home that cleverly blends into the background. It's hidden by the use of native stone, aged cedar siding, and the thick backdrop of evergreen and hardwood forest. For Richard and Patti Upton, not being seen, but being able to see out, was the idea all along.

In 1976 the Uptons commissioned Frank McGary, the architect with many local designs to his credit, to create this living environment. Using the spectacular setting of Eden Isle's rolling hills and expectation of daily postcard sunsets, the design captures the essence of the surroundings by direct involvement with the outdoors. He has made extensive use of floor-to-ceiling doors and windows, multi-level decks, and an open floorplan further illuminated by skylights.

The home is furnished in a Mediterranean style with a casual mix of Mexican and Spanish antiques. The unusual flooring is made of stained concrete squares, and several areas are topped with bright blue and white woven rugs.

Many of the furnishings in the kitchen came from La Posada in Monterrey, Mexico, one of Pancho Villa's favorite haunts. The Uptons even managed to track down the stools Villa sat in to watch cockfights. Woven baskets line the exposed rough-hewn beams above.

A few steps away in the dining area rests an extensively carved Mexican bench that was once owned by Carol Burnett. A nearby Mexican tile slab sideboard is supported by chiseled white stone blocks.

Rich, dark colorations and textures in all the furnishings, contrasting with white walls and streaming bursts of sunlight, deliver a strong lasting impression for any visitor.

Patti has collected the work of Heber Springs artists to continue the local environmental theme.

The home started out as a weekend retreat but has become a primary residence due in part to Patti's locally headquartered business. She is president and founder of Aromatique, Inc., the successful designer room fragrance products company. As you might expect, the home smells as good as it looks.

In 1988-89 the Uptons added almost 1,800 square feet to the original structure. They expanded with a master bedroom and bath, a new breakfast room and a three-tier deck with pool. Of course, the deck faces west to make it easy for all to experience the fabulous sunset panoramas.

Others must think that the setting has picture-perfect qualities, too. It's been seen in *Southern Living* and the *Memphis Commercial Appeal*.

EXTRAVAGANT GRANARY

A mix of family heirlooms and collectibles, this house offers the visitor visual shocks at every turn. It is an Alice in Wonderland approach to living, a major statement of color, unabashed frenzy of angles and complete disregard for architectural time frames. It's the home of painter Donald Roller Wilson and his wife Kathy.

He calls his home an "extravagant granary." The exterior is completely unpretentious – tin and brick, industrial bar joists and commercial windows, all manufactured in Arkansas. The front doors are commercial aluminum frame glass with white vinyl block letters proclaiming: "Specializing in the storage of all fine grains with the exception of creamed corn (whole kernel is OK)."

The flooring throughout the home is formed by a striking alternating pattern of black walnut and red oak, with perimeters of dark walnut, all custom milled by John Banks of Huntsville. This visual tension sets the scene for the interior's striking color scheme and the plethora of interesting accents.

An Italian Gothic Revival sofa, plucked from its original home in Rome, hugs one west wall. Rich-toned Clarence House coverings abound. Flea market finds are presented everywhere. Stone spheres, antique toy trucks and books line shelves in the study. Collections of Niloak Swirl pottery from Benton and Czechoslovakian art glass are also on display.

Kitchen tiles around the stove were designed by Kathy Thompson of Fayetteville. All appliances are restaurant quality and size, like the Wolf Range and Traulsen Refrigerator.

The tufted red leather kitchen dining booth is a quirky corner designed by Steve Marquardt and painted by his wife Gloria. The table features a shadowbox beneath glass, offering a peek at a fascinating jumble of objects.

The study houses collections of poetry and antique books in towering cases. The marble fireplace is from England by way of a Jonesboro home.

Wilson displays only one of his own paintings in his home. However, his works are in private collections across the country, including those of celebrities Dan Aykroyd, Carol Burnett, Douglas Cramer, Carrie Fisher, Eddie Fisher, Stacy Keach, Graham Nash, Mike Nichols, Jack Nicholson, Mary Kay Place, Debbie Reynolds, Diane Sawyer, Meryl Streep, Aaron Spelling, Elizabeth Taylor, Robin Williams and Frank Zappa.

The granary was designed by Rene Diaz of Lawrence, Kansas, (formerly of the University of Arkansas at Fayetteville faculty) and Harry Teague of Aspen, Colorado, and was constructed in 1988.

HIDDEN SPLENDOR

The exterior is an unadorned two-story plastered box, actually touching neighborhood sidewalks. Painted in a neutral taupe, it doesn't stop traffic. There are no clues to the splendor hidden behind the 14-inch-thick walls.

Located on lot one, block one of the original city of Pulaski Heights, this 1905 structure was once Witt's Grocery & Market. Deliveries were made by horse-drawn buggy. The family apartment was on the upper floor. Street-cars stopped here on their Pulaski Heights runs.

Several businesses occupied the Federal-style building until 1975 when it was purchased and totally rehabilitated by Victor Zanovich, ASID. Trans-forming a market into his grand home was a challenge, but Zanovich was equal to the task. He is an accomplished interior designer and has been practicing in Little Rock since 1953. Master craftsmen spent a full year making his dream a reality.

The treasures inside this urban jewel are a fitting collection for a man who has influenced the taste of so many. The living room's backdrop displays an impressive 12-panel Coromandel lacquered screen, circa 1794. The ten-foot-tall screen panels are joined by remarkable hand-made hinges.

Walls are endowed with traditional realist oil portraits and Italian land-scapes rendered in oil on copper. Amid the many collectibles shines a Fabergé snuff box.

The antique walnut paneled fireplace wall, transplanted from a home in Kentucky, is 200 years old and glows with history. And to top that, Victor employed local wood craftsmen to match, on site, the room's crown molding with the look and feel of the antique paneling.

The privacy and intimacy of this jewel box-like home are carried outside as you enter a small garden through French doors.

The Zanovich home has been featured in *Southern Accents* and has been used as the setting for a Dillard's Christmas catalog.

A TOUR OF THANKS

*Beyond the gracious homeowner support, many volunteer hours
and in-kind contributions have made this book a reality.*

Junior League of Little Rock, Inc.

1990-91 Private Tour Committee
Production and Marketing

Penelope Williams Rudder, Chairman
Jan Nelson Cooper, Business Manager
Hunter W. Gray, Consultant
Victoria Clement Garrett
Sharon Deckelman Mosley
Kelli Quinn Thomas
Sheb Adkisson Trotter
Carmen Holden McHaney, Arkansas Easter Seal Society Liaison

1989-90 Private Tour Committee
Project Development

Shelia Stricklin Vaught, Chairman
Penelope Williams Rudder, Co-Chairman
Jan Nelson Cooper, Business Manager
Hunter W. Gray, Consultant
Margaret Kelly Balch
Victoria Clement Garrett
Libby Darwin Grobmyer
Nancy Rather Kumpuris
Jo Retzloff Magee
Sharon Deckelman Mosley
Breda Avinchey Turner
Laura Camacho Hathaway, Arkansas Easter Seal Society Liaison

Junior League Presidents

Nancy Lanford Bishop, 1990-91 President
Mero Lindsey McCreery, 1989-90 President
Beth Eldredge McCain, 1988-89 President

Arkansas Easter Seal Society

Mary Wilson Allison, Director of Development
Jim Butler, Executive Director
Michael C. Schaufele, President of the Board of Directors

Additional Acknowledgements

Diversified Graphics, Inc.
Jungkind Photo-graphic
Peerless Engravers
Peerless Photographic
Robert L. Robinson, Jr., Robinson, Staley & Marshall

*Murfee – Oakland
El Dorado*